BadBoy Food
https://www.badboyfood.net/

info@badboyfood.net

What's Inside

A LITTLE BIT FROM ME

First, let me thank you for buying this awesome book. Not only are you on your way to making some badboy burgers, but you are also giving something back to charity at the same time as I always donate some of the profits from my cookbooks to charity.

I have always had a passion for food. Food for me is not just nourishment, it is much more. Whether it be fine dining, pizza, curry, barbeque, or a simple sandwich, it has to great, and there is no excuse for it not to be. For food to be great, it does not require expensive ingredients or years of training. It takes love and passion and an unwavering belief that you will not settle for anything that is not great, anything that is not badboy.

I am constantly on various food missions to find and create great food, and this book is no different. I wanted to create some easy to follow recipes that allow all of us to make the kind of burger we wish we got when we go out to eat. The kind of burger that literally gives you goosebumps when you bite into it, and I reckon the badboy burgers in this book do just that.

Feel free to give feedback about how the dishes can be improved, and I will try to include those ideas in future versions of the book.

NOW LET'S MAKE SOME BADBOY BURGERS!

WHAT IS A BADBOY BURGER?

A badboy burger, like all badboy food, is not about the chef being a badboy: it is about the ingredients and final product being badboy. It is a burger that doesn't mess around. It uses the best ingredients to produce the best possible burger: no soggy buns that fall apart, no pre-ground meat from 100 different animals, no wilted lettuce, and no fake processed cheese. Just real hearty ingredients to create real hearty food.

BECOME A BADBOY FOODIE

If you would like to join the badboy food movement and spread the love of badboy food, head over to **badboyfood.net/foodie**. You will receive exclusive updates and offers and join a community of like-minded foodies.

HOW TO SHAPE YOUR BURGERS

THE BURGER PRESS

One way to shape your burgers is to use a burger press. They are quite cheap to buy and they provide a nice uniformed shape to each patty. There are many different styles of press, but the idea is the same. Just push the meat into the base until flat, and then push the top down until you have a nice compact buger.

SHAPE BY HAND

Some people prefer to shape their burgers by themselves as they don't like the uniformed shape from the burger press. Just get the meat and roll it into a ball in your hand. Then push it out on the worksurface to create the size and shape burger of your choice.

SQUISH IN THE PAN

If you don't want the uniformed shape of the burger press or even the burger shaped by hand, you can go for the squish in the pan option. Just roll the meat into a ball, slap it in the pan, and push it flat with your hand, a spatular, or a burger weight.

HOW TO COOK YOUR BURGERS

THE PAN

The most important thing to do when getting ready to cook burgers is to make sure that your pan is super hot. A cast-iron pan or griddle is the best choice as it loses less heat when you put the burger on than other pans.

1ST SIDE

With your pan super hot (smoking), either place your burger in the pan or squish it down and watch it sizzle. If it doesn't sizzle, your pan is not hot enough. I like my burgers medium-rare. It needs to be cooked enough for the fat to start to render, and you get a really juicy burger. Cook this first side for about 3-4 minutes. Do not move it before this time. You want to form a good crust underneath first.

2ND SIDE

Once the first side has a good crust and has been cooking for 3-4 minutes, flip it over and cook for the same time on the other side. Now is when you add cheese if the recipe requires it. The cheese will be perfect melted when the burger is cooked.

THE BUNS

When you flip the burger is when you should start to toast your buns. Slice them and place them flat side down in the same pan as the burgers. To really get the shiny look to them. You can cover the pan with a lid and allow the steam and fat of the burgers to coat the tops of the buns. Be careful not to burn them.

A BIT OF MEAT

11

THE ULTIMATE BADBOY

INGREDIENTS

1½ lbs ground beef (15-20% fat)

¼ pound of Cheddar cheese

5 slices of bacon

1 lettuce

5 burger buns

6 slices dill pickle

2 tomatoes (sliced)

1 red onion (sliced & separated into rings)

Ketchup

Mustard

THE COOK

Divide the beef into five pieces. prepare the patties in your prefered way (see page 7)

Cook your bacon until crisp, set to one side and wipe the pan clean of bacon fat.

Cook the patties and buns (see page 9)

Add a couple of slices of the cheddar cheese when you start cooking the second side of the patties. It should be melted by the time the burger is cooked.

THE BUILD

Spread the mustard on the bottom of the bun and add the burger.

Add the lettuce, 2 slices of tomato and a few rings of onion.

Spread the ketchup on the inside of the top bun. Get stuck in!

PORTOBELLO & GOAT CHEESE ON BEEF

INGREDIENTS

1½ lbs ground beef (15-20% fat)

¼ cup olive oil

2 tbsp. balsamic vinegar

1 tbsp. rosemary

2 cloves garlic (mashed)

5 portobello mushrooms

½ cup goat cheese

1 ½ cups baby spinach leaves

3 tbsp. mayonnaise

2 cloves garlic, minced

2 limes (juiced)

5 burger buns

THE COOK

Divide the beef into five pieces. prepare the patties in your prefered way (see page 7)

Mix half of the garlic and all of the lime juice from the limes with the mayonnaise.

Mix, rosemary, vinegar, olive oil and half the garlic in a bowl.

Brush the mushroom caps with the oil and garlic mixture and start frying them for 5 minutes on both sides.

Cook the patties and the buns (see page 9)

When you flip the patties, put a slice of the goat's cheese on top of the burger.

The burger and the mushrooms should be ready at the same time.

THE BUILD

Lay the spinach on the bottom of the bun.

Follow this with the burger.

Lay the mushroom on the burger.

Spread the garlic mayonnaise inside the top bun.

Get stuck in!

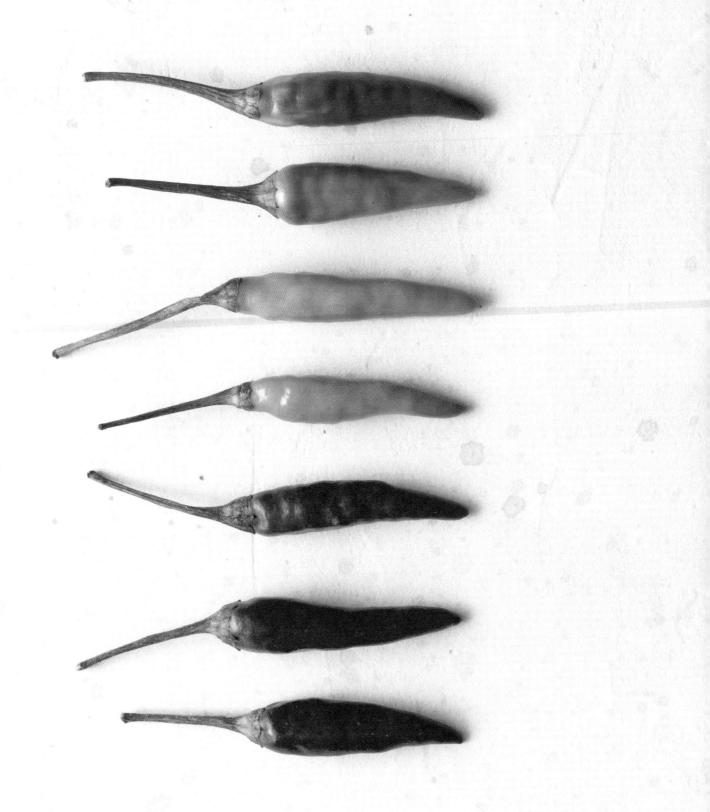

THE SPICY THAI with Nahm Jim Mayo

INGREDIENTS

THE PATTY

1½ lbs ground beef (15-20% fat)

2 tbsp. lemon grass (ground very fine)

2 tbsp. fresh basil (finely chopped)

2 tbsp. shallots (finely chopped)

2 red chili peppers (finely chopped)

¼ cup peanuts (finely chopped)

Salt and pepper

Handful of cilantro/coriander (torn)

NAHM JIM MAYO

1½ tsp. fish sauce

1½ tsp. lime juice

1½ tsp. uncooked white rice

½ cup of chopped cilantro (coriander)

½ cup of mayonnaise

1 tsp. chili flakes

THE COOK

Roast the rice in a dry frying pan or a dish in the oven until it has browned.

Once it has cooled, use a pestle and mortar or spice crusher to crush it to a semi-fine powder.

Mix the ground rice and the remaining nahm jim mayo ingredients together and put to one side.

Mix all of the patty ingredients, except the lime, salt and pepper in a bowl.

Divide the beef mixture into five pieces.

Prepare the patties in your prefered way (see page 7).

Cook the patties and the buns (see page 9).

THE BUILD

Lay a good handful of cilantro on the bottom bun.

Add the patty.

Spread lashings of the nahm jim mayo on the top bun.

Get stuck in!

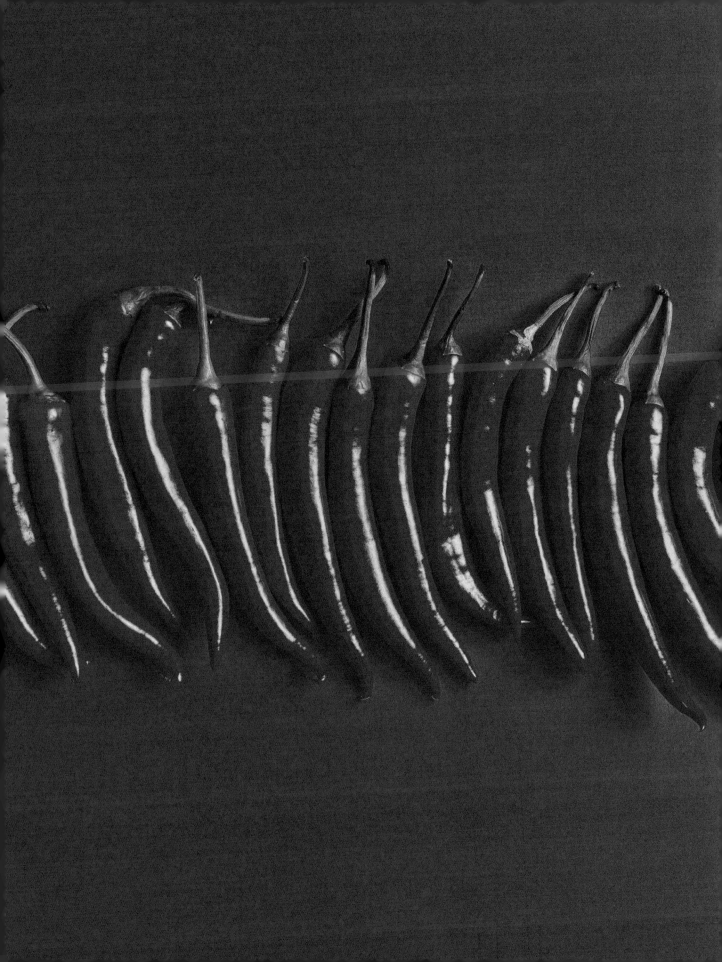

PICANTE BEEF

INGREDIENTS

1½ lbs ground beef (15-20% fat)

5 burger buns

¼ pound strong cheddar

Lettuce & tomato for a bit of colour if needed

PICANTE SAUCE

5 chipotle peppers (dried)

1 cup of tomatoes (chopped)

1 cup of jalapeno peppers (chopped)

½ an onion (chopped)

2 garlic cloves (chopped)

1½ tbsp. cilantro (chopped)

½ tbsp. cayenne powder

½ tbsp. cumin (ground)

¼ cup water

1 tsp. salt

1 tsp. pepper

⅓ cup cider vinegar

Juice ½ lime

THE COOK

Add the Picante sauce ingredients to a blender and blend fully. Add to a saucepan, bring to the boil and simmer for 15 minutes. Towards the end of the 15 minutes, start the burgers.

Divide the beef mixture into five pieces. Prepare the patties in your prefered way (see page 7)

Cook the patties and the buns (see page 9)

When you flip the patties to cook the second side, add a couple of slices of cheddar. They should be melted by the time the burger is cooked.

THE BUILD

Add lettuce and tomato, if needed, to the bottom of the bun

Add the burger.

Generously cover with the picante sauce

Get stuck in!

SWISS CHEESE ON BEEF

INGREDIENTS

1½ pounds ground beef (15-20% fat)

10 slices of bacon

1 cup sweet onions (sliced)

1 cup mushrooms (sliced)

1 tsp. garlic (minced)

3 tsp. Dijon mustard

1 cup arugula (rocket)

¼ pound Swiss cheese Ingredients

THE COOK

Divide the beef mixture into five pieces.
Prepare the patties in your prefered way (see page 7).

Fry the bacon until brown and then remove from the pan. in the bacon fat. Fry the onions and mushrooms until soft and browned

At the same time, cook the patties and buns (see page 9).

When you flip the patty, put a slice or two of the Swiss cheese on top.

The burger and the mushrooms should be ready at the same time.

THE BUILD

Spread the mustard on the bottom of the bun.

Add the arugula to the mustard.

Add the patty.

Top with the bacon, mushrooms and onions.

Get stuck in!

KANSAS CITY STYLE

INGREDIENTS

THE BURGER

1½ lbs ground beef (15-20% fat)

2 tsp. garlic powder

2½ tsps. paprika

1 tsp. onion powder

1 tsp. cayenne pepper

1¼ tsp. dried oregano

1¼ tsp. dried thyme

½ tsp. red chili flakes

½ pound cheddar cheese

THE GREENS

2 cups collard greens (chopped)

2 cloves garlic (mince)

Olive oil

3 slices bacon

1 small onion (chopped)

2 cloves garlic (minced)

Salt & pepper

3 cups chicken broth

THE BARBECUE SAUCE

2 cups tomato pasata

½ smoked paprika

½ sweet paprika

1 tsp. cayenne pepper

¼ cup brown sugar

1 tbsp. chilli powder

1 tbsp. salt

1 tbsp. pepper

2 cups water

½ cup cider vinegar

6 garlic cloves chopped

3 tbsp olive oil

THE COOK

THE GREENS

Fry the bacon until crispy and add the onions, greens and garlic until they are nice and soft. Add salt, pepper and red pepper flakes to taste. Add the chicken stock and simmer for 45 minutes or until tender.
Strain the broth and cover to keep warm.

THE BARBECUE SAUCE

Fry the spices in the oil. Then add all of the other ingredients and simmer.

THE BURGER

Prepare and cook the patties and buns. (see pages 7 & 9). Add a couple of slices of the cheddar cheese when you start cooking the second side.

THE BUILD

On the bottom bun, place some of the well-strained greens. Add the burger. Then generous amounts of the barbecue sauce. Get stuck in!

THE CHEESY ITALIAN

(Gorgonzola with Balsamic Caramelized Onions and Pears on Beef)

INGREDIENTS

THE PATTIES

1½ lbs ground beef (15-20% fat)

1½ tsps. salt

1½ tsps. cracked black pepper

1½ tsps. dried parsley

1½ tsps. dried basil

1 tsp. dried fennel seed (ground)

½ teaspoon dried oregano

½ teaspoon dried thyme

THE ONIONS & PEARS

1 large onion (chopped)

2 pears (chopped)

½ cup balsamic vinegar

1 tbsp. Butter

Olive oil

THE REST

½ pound of gorgonzola

1 cup of arugula (rocket)

THE COOK

Mix all of the dry ingredients into the beef and divide into 5 pieces.

Prepare the patties in your prefered way (see page 7)

Boil the balsamic vinegar in a saucepan until it has reduced by half and allow it to cool and thicken. In a separate pan, fry the onions and pears in butter on a medium heat until they have browned. Then simmer until tender. Finish by adding the vinegar and season with salt to taste.

Prepare the patties in your prefered way (see page 7)

Cook the patties and the buns (see page 9)

THE BUILD

Spread the mustard on the bottom of the bun. Add the arugula to the mustard and the patty. Top with the bacon, mushrooms and onions. Get stuck in!

CHEESEY CHILLI

INGREDIENTS

THE BURGER

1½ lbs ground beef (15-20% fat)

Salt & pepper to taste

THE CHILLI

1 pound beef (ground)

1 onion (chopped)

1 red pepper (chopped)

14-ounce jar of passata

1 tsp. paprika

1 tsp. cumin (ground)

2 tbsp. tomato puree

14-ounce can of red kidney beans
(drained and rinsed)

1 tbsp. chili powder

3 garlic cloves (mashed)

THE REST

½ pound of strong cheddar cheese
(grated)

½ cup of sour cream

THE COOK

Prepare the patties in your prefered way (see page 7)

Fry the onion, red pepper, garlic, chili powder, cumin and paprika on a medium heat until the onions are soft. Add the beef and fry until the beef has started to brown. Add the beans, passata and tomato puree. Bring to the boil, and then simmer for 1 hour, or until nice and reduced.

Cook the patties and the buns (see page 9)

THE BUILD

Add the burger to the bottom bun.

Spoon on generous amounts of the chilli.

Add a good handful of grated cheese.

Finish with a nice serving of sour cream.

Get stuck in!

THE BEEFY ITALIAN

INGREDIENTS

THE BURGER

1½ lbs ground beef (15-20% fat)

½ tbsp. salt

½ tbsp. freshly cracked black pepper

½ tbsp. dried parsley

½ tbsp. dried basil

1 tsp. dried fennel seed (ground)

½ teaspoon dried oregano

½ teaspoon dried thyme

THE SAUCE

2 cups fresh basil

2 sprigs fresh oregano

2 sprigs marjoram

1 sprig rosemary

1 sprig thyme

1 cup Mayonnaise

1 lemon

¼ cup sundried tomatoes (chopped)

¼ cup artichokes (drained and chopped)

¼ roasted pepper (chopped)

PESTO MAYO

1 cup fresh basil leaves

2 cloves garlic, peeled

1½ tbsp. pine nuts

⅓ cup Parmesan cheese

Salt and pepper, to taste

½ cup olive oil

½ cup mayonnaise

THE REST

½ lb mozzarella cheese

2 tomatoes

5 burger buns

THE COOK

Mix all of the sauce ingredients together. It should not be too runny.

Blend the pesto mayo ingredients together, except the mayonnaise. Then mix the blended ingredients with the mayonnaise.

Mix all of the beef ingredients together.

Prepare the patties in your preferred way (see page 7)

Cook the patties and the buns (see page 9)

THE BUILD

Spread some pesto mayo on the bottom bun and then add the patty.

Tear some cheese apart and add to the burger.

Add some fresh basil and a couple of tomato slices.

Add generous amounts of sauce.

Get stuck in!

THE ENGLISH BREAKFAST

INGREDIENTS

1 ½ pound ground beef (15-20% fat)

5 organic eggs (they just taste nicer)

5 strips of bacon

1 black pudding sausage (sliced)

1 tomato (sliced)

1 cup of mushrooms, should be white, but I prefer wild (sliced)

14-ounce tin baked beans

Tomato sauce

Brown sauce

Salt & pepper

THE COOK

Prepare the patties in your prefered way (see page 7). Get at least two frying pans ready and a saucepan. Now, take some deep breaths. This will all happen very quickly. Heat the beans in a saucepan until boiling. Try to fry everything that follows at the same time. Heat some oil on a medium heat and fry the mushrooms, tomatoes and black pudding until cooked through and the bacon until it is crispy. Fry the eggs and tomatoes until the tomatoes are cooked through and the eggs are done (it's better if the eggs are sunny side up) Cook the patties and the buns (see page 9)

THE BUILD

Spread some brown sauce on the bottom bun. Add some mushrooms, the burger and then the tomato. Spoon on some beans. Add a few slices of bacon and black pudding. Finish with a egg and some tomato sauce. Get stuck in!

A
LITTLE
PIGGY

PORKY THAI LARB

INGREDIENTS

THE BURGER

1½ lbs ground beef (15-20% fat)

½ -1 tbsp. chili flakes

2 tbsp. finely chopped lemongrass

½ tbsp. of fish sauce

1 - 2 limes (juice)

2 shallots (finely chopped)

½ cup of chopped cilantro (coriander)

4 spring onions (finely chopped)

½ cup of mint (finely chopped)

½ cup rice

THE SAUCE

½ cup of ripped cilantro (coriander)

½ cup of mint (ripped)

1 cup mayonnaise

2 tsp. chili powder

½ lime (juice)

1 tbsp. roasted rice

THE REST

½ cup of ripped cilantro (coriander)

½ cup of mint (ripped)

2 shallots (sliced)

THE COOK

Roast the rice in a dry frying pan or a dish in the oven until it has browned.

Once it has cooled, use a pestle and mortar or spice crusher to crush it to a semi-fine powder.

In a bowl, gently mix 2 tbsp. of the rice powder with the beef, chili flakes, lemongrass, fish sauce, lime juice, shallots, cilantro and mint.

Divide the beef mixture into 5 pieces.

Prepare the patties in your prefered way (see page 7)

Cook the patties and the buns. (see page 9)

THE BUILD

Place the patty on the bottom bun.

Add a some of the shallots, mint and cilantro.

Spoon on generous helpings of the sauce.

Get stuck in!

SPICY ITALIAN PORK

INGREDIENTS

THE PATTIES

1½ lbs ground pork (15-20% fat)

½ tbsp. salt

½ tbsp. freshly cracked black pepper

½ tbsp. dried parsley

½ tbsp. dried basil

1 tsp. ground fennel seed

½ tsp. dried oregano

½ tsp. dried thyme

2 tsp. cayenne pepper

2 tsp. paprika

1 tsp. smoked paprika

1 tsp. chili flakes

THE SAUCE

Olive oil

1 large onion (sliced)

½ green & bell pepper (sliced)

½ red bell pepper (sliced)

Salt & pepper

2 cloves garlic (chopped)

½ sprig fresh oregano (chopped)

1 sprig fresh thyme (chopped)

8 ounces passata

¼ cup red wine

Handful basil (chopped)

THE REST

½ pound provolone cheese

1 cup of arugula (rocket)

2 tomatoes

5 ciabatta rolls

THE COOK

Mix all of the beef ingredients together, and prepare the patties (see page 7)

For the sauce, fry the onions and peppers on a medium heat until they soften. Add the rest of the sauce ingredients and simmer on a low heat until it has reduced to form a thick sauce.

Cook the patties and the buns (see page 9)

Add some slices of cheese when you flip them.

THE BUILD

Lay some arugula on the bottom of the bun. Add a few slices of tomato. Add the burger. Spoon on generous amounts of the sauce. Get stuck in!

PULLED PORK

INGREDIENTS

2 lbs pork shoulder/collar

1 large onion sliced

Salt and ground black pepper

BARBECUE SAUCE

2 cups tomato pasata

½ smoked paprika

½ sweet paprika

1 tsp. cayenne pepper

¼ cup brown sugar

1 tbsp. chili powder

1 tbsp. salt

1 tbsp. pepper

2 cups water

½ cup cider vinegar

6 garlic cloves chopped

3 tbsp olive oil

THE COOK

THE PORK

Season the pork with salt a pepper. Not too much, just a slight covering. You can also rub in some of the same spices from the barbecue sauce, but I just go with salt and pepper. Place in a dutch oven or another ovenproof dish with a lid a cook at 130F for 4-8 hours, or until it falls apart when you full it with a fork. When the pork is cooked, take it out of the oven, remove the lid, cover it with foil and let rest for at least an hour. Then pull apart with two forks adding some of the barbecue sauce as you do. Then fry the onion in some of the pork juices.

THE BARBECUE SAUCE

Towards the end of the pork cooking time, fry the spices in the oil. Then add all of the other ingredients and simmer until nice and thick.

THE BUILD

Add generous helpings of the pork to the bottom bun. Followed by the onions and more of the sauce.

Get stuck in!

CHEEKY
LAMB

INDIAN LAMB

INGREDIENTS

1½ lbs ground lamb (15-20% fat)

3/4 tsp. ginger mashed up

3/4 tsp. garlic mashed up

3 tsp. garam masala

1 ½ teaspoon fresh chopped cilantro (coriander)

½ cup fresh yoghurt

¼ cup fresh mint (chopped)

½ cup of ripped arugula (rocket)

5 burger buns

THE COOK

Mix the mint and yoghurt together and place to one side.

Mix the lamb, ginger, garlic, garam masala and cilantro in a bowl.

Prepare the patties in your prefered way (see page 7).

Cook the patties and the buns. (see page 9).

THE BUILD

Place the ripped arugula on the bottom of the buns, and then add the patties.

Spread generous amounts of the yoghurt and mint sauce on the inside of the top of the bun.

Get stuck in!

MAPLE GLAZED LAMB & GOAT'S CHEESE

INGREDIENTS

THE PATTIES

1½ lbs ground lamb (15-20% fat)

¼ lb soft goat cheese

2 sprigs of fresh rosemary (chopped)

2 tbsp. maple syrup

1 ½ tsp. salt

½ tsp. black pepper (cracked)

1 head garlic

1 tbsp. olive oil

THE CHEESE

2 tbsp. maple syrup

¼ lb soft goat cheese

THE REST

1 packet of arugula (rocket)

5 burger buns

THE COOK

Mix the patty ingredients together.

Mix the cheese with the maple syrup.

Prepare the patties in your prefered way (see page 7).

Cook the patties and the buns. (see page 9).

While cooking each side, drizzle maple syrup.

THE BUILD

Place the ripped arugula on the bottom of the buns and then add the patties.

Spread generous amounts of the cheese and maple syrup mix on top.

Get stuck in!

SPICED LAMB

INGREDIENTS

THE PATTIES

1½ lbs ground lamb (15-20% fat)

2 tbsp. fresh mint leaves (chopped)

2 tbsp. fresh cilantro (chopped)

2 tbsp. fresh oregano (chopped)

1 tbsp. garlic, chopped

1 tsp. ground cumin

¼ tsp. ground allspice

½ tsp. chili flakes

½ tsp. salt

½ tsp. ground black pepper

THE REST

½ cup plain yoghurt

2 tbsp. fresh mint leaves (chopped)

5 burger buns

1 cup arugula (rocket)

½ pound feta cheese

THE COOK

Mix the patty ingredients together.

Prepare the patties in your prefered way (see page 7).

Mix the yogurt and the mint together.

Cook the patties and the buns. (see page 9).

THE BUILD

Add the patties to the bottom of the buns.

Then place the ripped arugula.

Drizzle generous amounts of the minty yogurt on top.

Crumble some feta cheese.

Get stuck in!

A BIT
OF BIRD

MEXICAN CHICKEN

INGREDIENTS

THE CHICKEN

5 skinless chicken breasts

3 tbsp. olive oil

2 tbsp. lemon juice

1 tsp. seasoned salt

1½ tsp. dried oregano

1½ tsp. ground cumin

1 tsp. garlic powder

½ tsp. chili powder

½ tsp. smoked paprika

½ tsp. red pepper flakes

THE GUACAMOLE

3 ripe avocados (peeled with no stones)

1 tomato (diced)

1 small onion (diced)

2 limes

Bunch of cilantro

1 tbsp. olive oil

Salt

THE SALSA

3 tomatoes (diced)

½ small onion (diced)

1 lime

1 bunch of cilantro

Olive oil

Salt & Pepper

Extras

Sour cream

Cilantro

THE COOK

Mix all of the chicken ingredients together. Add the chicken breasts and make sure they are well covered in the spice and oil mixture. Place in the refrigerator.

For the Guacamole, mash the avocado in a bowl and mix in the tomatoes, onions, cilantro, one tablespoon of olive oil and the juice from 1½ limes. Add salt to taste and more lime or oil as needed.

Fort the salsa, mix the tomatoes, onions, cilantro, one tablespoon of olive oil and the juice from the lime in a bowl. Add salt and pepper to taste and more limes or oil as needed.

Fry the chicken breasts until cooked through. Heat the buns.

THE BUILD

Lay some arugula on the bottom of the bun. Add a few slices of tomato. Add the burger. Spoon on generous amounts of the sauces. Get stuck in!

INDIAN CHICKEN

INGREDIENTS

THE PATTIES

1¼ lbs ground chicken
4 large garlic cloves
½ tsp. salt
½ tsp. black pepper
1 tsp. ground coriander
½ tsp. ground cumin
¼ tsp. ground cinnamon
1/8 tsp. ground cloves
10 oz. spinach (pre-
cooked and well-
strained)
2 tbsp. minced ginger
1 jalapeno pepper,
seeded and minced

The Sauce

½ large cucumber, (diced
very small)
¼ tsp. ground cumin
1 tbsp. fresh lime juice
Salt & Pepper to Taste

THE REST

¼ cup mango chutney
½ pound paneer cheese
¼ cup of yogurt
Lettuce leaves
2 tomatoes (sliced)
1 onion (slices)
5 burger buns

THE COOK

Mix all of the patty ingredients together, and
prepare the patties (see page 7).
For the sauce, in a blender, blend the lime
juice, cucumber, ¼ tsp. cumin, yoghurt and
add salt to taste.
Cook the patties and the buns. (see page 9).
Add some paneer cheese when you cook the
second side.

THE BUILD

Lay a few pieces of lettuce, tomato and
rings of onion onto the bottom.
Lay the chicken patty on top.
Spoon a generous amount of the
yoghurt mixture on top.
Add chutney and the top bun.
Get stuck in!

THE SUNDAY ROAST

INGREDIENTS

THE CHICKEN

1 chicken

Olive oil

Handful of fresh thyme (chopped)

Handful of fresh oregano (chopped)

Handful of fresh rosemary (chopped)

Salt & Pepper

The Vegies

5 potatoes (peeled)

2 carrots

1 small pumpkin/squash

2 tbsp. duck fat or lard

2 tbsp. butter

The Gravy

1 glass red wine

200ml chicken stock

2 tbsp. plain flour

Fresh rosemary, thyme and sage

THE VEGIES

5 potatoes (peeled)

2 carrots

1 small pumpkin/squash

2 tbsp. duck fat or lard

2 tbsp. butter

The Bread Sauce

1 onion

5 cloves

2 bay leaves

40g butter

Pinch nutmeg (finely grated)

6 peppercorns

3 tbsp. think cream

600ml milk

100g breadcrumbs (white)

The Rest

Burger Buns

THE SUNDAY ROAST

THE COOK

THE CHICKEN

Preheat the oven to 240°C/475°F.

Turn the chicken over and cut it down the middle from top to bottom with a sharp knife.

Turn it back over again and push it down, so it lays flat open on the surface. This is so it can cook quicker than a usual roast

Rub the chicken with the olive and herbs and leave to stand at room temperature for about 30 minutes.

THE POTATOES

Add the duck fat/lard and the butter to a roasting pan and place it in the oven.

Cut the potatoes into 1 inch to 1½ inches thick pieces.

Boil them in lightly salted water for 5-10 minutes or until they are slightly soft on the outside but not soft in the middle.

Strain them and then shake them in the strainer to make them fluffy.

Add the potatoes to the preheated roasting pan of fat and butter. Be careful it will spit?

Make sure the potatoes are covered by the oil.

Cook for about an hour or until golden brown.

Turn the potatoes every 20 minutes to ensure an even cook.

After about 45 minutes, add some fresh rosemary, thyme, sage and whole garlic cloves.

THE VEGETABLES (PUT IN ABOUT 20 MINUTES AFTER THE POTATOES)

Toss the vegetables gently in a bowl with olive oil, salt and pepper.

Lay the vegetables on a baking tray. Make sure they are not on top of each other.

Place in the oven and roast for about 45 minutes or until golden brown.

THE SUNDAY ROAST

The Chicken (put in about 20 minutes after the veg)

Place the chicken on a roasting tray, and put it in the oven. Immediately reduce the heat to 200C/390F. Regularly baste the chicken with its own juices to keep it moist. Cooking time depends on the chicken size. To check if it is cooked, cut between the leg and breast. If the juices run clear, it is cooked. Also, if you can pull the leg meat off with your fingers, it is cooked. When done, remove it from the tray and keep it warm. Keep the tray for the gravy.

Bread Sauce (start when the chicken goes in the oven)

Pierce the onion with the cloves and place in a saucepan with the milk, cream, peppercorns and bay leaves. Bring to the boil and then simmer for 15 minutes. Sieve the mixture and return the milk to the saucepan. Slowly stir in the breadcrumbs, and then add the nutmeg, butter and salt to taste. Just before serving, heat and add more milk if it's too thick. Slice the burger buns and lightly grill them.

THE GRAVY

Place the chicken roasting dish on the hob and heat it. Add the wine and chicken stock, fresh rosemary, thyme and sage and bring to the boil. Using a fork or whisk, scrape all of the roasted chicken bits from the bottom of the tray and mix with the gravy. Reduce the gravy by half. Slowly mix in a few tablespoons of flour until it had reached the desired thickness. Add salt to taste. Sieve to remove the bit. Leave to settle and then remove the top layer of oil.

THE BUILD

Spread a generous amount of bread sauce on the bottom bun. Tear a healthy portion of chicken (including the skin) and place it on the sauce. Add some of the vegetables and roast potatoes. Finish with a few good spoons of gravy. Get stuck in!

A LITTLE LESS MEATY

Veggie time!

FALAFEL

Yogurt & Dill Sauce

INGREDIENTS

THE FALAFEL

2 x 400g can chickpeas
(drained and rinsed)
4 garlic cloves (chopped)
Good handful parsley
Good Handful of cilantro
(coriander)
¾ large onion (chopped)
2 tsp. ground cumin
1 tsp. chili powder
4 tbsp. plain flour
1½ tsp. salt
¼ tsp. Black pepper
Sunflower oil for frying

THE SALSA

3 tomatoes (diced)
½ small onion (diced)
1 lime
1 bunch of cilantro
Olive oil
Salt & Pepper

THE SAUCE

1 cup plain yoghurt
1 clove garlic
2 tsp. extra virgin olive oil
1-2 limes (juice)
2 tbsp. fresh dill (chopped)

THE REST

5 burger buns
Good handful of arugula
(rocket)
400g humus

THE COOK

Blend the falafel ingredients (not the oil). Shape the mixture into 5 patties.

Mix the salsa ingredients. Add salt and pepper to taste and more limes or oil as needed.

Mix all Ingredients for the sauce in a bowl and chill until needed.

Shallow fry the patties in the oil until golden brown all over. Turn regularly to achieve an even cook. When they are nearly done, slice your buns and heat each side in the same pan as the patties

THE BUILD

Place some arugula on the bottom bun. Then the patty. Spoon on a good helping of the salsa. Drizzle some sauce. Get stuck in!

ROASTED VEGETABLE

INGREDIENTS

2 red bell peppers

2 green bell peppers

3 tomatoes

1 small pumpkin/squash

3 large onions

Extra virgin olive oil

½ pound cheddar (grated)

5 burger buns

THE COOK

Preheat the oven to 425F / 220C

Slice the peppers lengthwise in quarters and remove the seeds.

Half the tomatoes and remove the seeds.

Slice the pumpkin into 1-inch slices.

Cut the onions into quarters.

Toss the vegetables gently in a bowl with olive oil, salt and pepper.

Lay the vegetables on a baking tray. Make sure they are not on top of each other.

Place in the oven and roast for about 45 minutes or until golden brown.

Towards the end of the cooking time, lightly grill your buns.

THE BUILD

Layer your vegetables on the bottom bun until they have reached your desired thickness.

Add generous amounts of cheese.

Get stuck in!

A BIT ON THE SIDE

AVOCADO FRIES

INGREDIENTS

4 ripe avocados

2 cups bread crumbs

1 lime (juiced)

½ cup flour

Salt & Pepper

4 tbsp. extra virgin olive oil

1 egg

THE COOK

Preheat the oven to 400F/200C

Remove the flesh from the avocados and slice them about ¾ inch thick. Whisk the egg in a bowl. Place the flour in a bowl. Place the breadcrumbs in a bowl. Dip the avocado slices in the flour and then the egg and finally cover in the breadcrumbs. Place on an oiled baking tray. Sprinkle some more of the oil on top of the avocado. Place in the oven for 20-25 minutes or until golden brown.

GARLIC AND PARMESAN FRIES

INGREDIENTS

4 potatoes

Handful of oregano (chopped)

Handful of sage (chopped)

Handful of thyme (chopped)

½ cup of parmesan cheese (grated)

1 tsp. garlic powder

Olive oil

THE COOK

Wash the potatoes and cut them into fries.

Bol in water for 3-5 minutes, depending on thickness. Strain and then dry on a kitchen towel.

Fry in oil at 360F/180C until golden brown. Sieve the fries and leave to dry on some kitchen towel.

Spread the fries on a baking tray and sprinkle the parmesan, thyme, oregano, garlic powder and sage over them and toss until fully covered.

Grill until the cheese is golden.

CHEESY FRIES

INGREDIENTS

4 potatoes
½ lb. mature cheddar
(grated)

THE COOK

Wash the potatoes and cut them into fries.
Bol in water for 3-5 minutes, depending on thickness.
Strain and then dry on a kitchen towel.
Fry in oil at 360F/180C until golden brown. Sieve the
fries and leave to dry on some kitchen towel.
Spread the fries on a baking tray and sprinkle the
cheese and grill until the cheese is golden.

PARMESAN ZUCCHINI FRIES

INGREDIENTS

A handful of zucchini
Handful of oregano (chopped)
Handful of sage (chopped)
Handful of thyme (chopped)
½ cup of parmesan cheese
1-2 cups breadcrumbs
1 cup of flour
2 eggs
Olive oil

THE COOK

Slice the zucchini into fries and whisk the egg in a
bowl. Mix the herbs, cheese and flour and place in a
bowl. Place the breadcrumbs in a bowl. Dip the
zucchini slices in the flour and then the egg and
finally cover with the cheese & breadcrumbs mixture.
Place on a baking sheet + tray that has been oiled
with the olive oil. Sprinkle some more of the oil on
top. Cook in the oven at 400F/200C until golden
brown.

SWEET POTATO WEDGES

INGREDIENTS

5 sweet potatoes

1 tsp. Cumin

2 tsp. Roasted chili flakes

½ cup of thyme (chopped)

½ cup of rosemary (chopped)

2 cloves garlic (mashed)

2 tbsp. olive oil

THE COOK

Wash and peel the potatoes and slice them into 1½ inch wedges. Blend the herbs and the oil into a paste and cover the potatoes in it. Bake in the oven in a roasting pan at 400F/200C until brown.

Sprinkle with salt and serve.

GARLIC AND PARMESAN WEDGES

INGREDIENTS

5 potatoes

Handful of oregano (chopped)

Handful of sage (chopped)

Handful of thyme (chopped)

½ cup of parmesan cheese (grated)

1 tsp. garlic powder

Olive oil

THE COOK

Wash the potatoes and cut them into wedges. Bol in water for 5-10 minutes, depending on thickness. Strain and then dry on a kitchen towel. Toss in oil and bake in an oven in a roasting pan at 400F/200C for about 25 minutes. Sprinkle the parmesan, thyme, oregano, garlic powder and sage over the potatoes and toss until fully covered.

Return to the oven and cook for a further 10 minutes or until golden brown.

SPICY CORN

INGREDIENTS

5 ears corn (husked)

½ cup mayonnaise

1 tbsp. chili powder

1 tbsp. smoked paprika

1 cup feta cheese (crumbled)

2 limes

Salt

THE COOK

Brush the corn with the oil and grill on a medium heat until it is slightly charred.

Sprinkle the chili, paprika, and cheese over the corn.

Squeeze some fresh lime.

ONION RINGS IN BEER BATTER

INGREDIENTS

3 cups all-purpose flour

1 egg, beaten

Salt and pepper to taste

1 cup beer (experiment with different types)

3 large onions (sliced to make rings)

Sunflower oil

THE COOK

In a bowl, mix 2 cups of flour, the egg and some salt and pepper to taste. Slowly whisk in the beer to your desired consistency. Place the remaining flour in a bowl.

Heat your oil in a saucepan or fryer to 375F/190C

Dip your onion rings in the flour and then in the batter, and then fry until golden.

Dab dry on some kitchen towel.

Serve hot with your chosen dipping sauce.

SAUCY DIPS

CILANTRO & LIME

INGREDIENTS

1 cup sour cream

½ cilantro (chopped)

2 tbsp. lime juice

Salt to taste

½ tsp. Garlic (minced)

THE COOK

Mix all Ingredients in a bowl.
You're done!

HONEY MUSTARD

INGREDIENTS

½ cup mayonnaise

¼ cup Dijon mustard

2 tbsp. honey

½ tbsp. lime juice

½ tsp. cayenne pepper

THE COOK

Mix all Ingredients in a bowl.
You're done!

GUACAMOLE

INGREDIENTS

3 ripe avocados

1 tomato (diced)

1 small onion (diced)

2 limes

Bunch of cilantro

Olive oil

Salt

THE COOK

Mash the avocado in a bowl and mix in the tomatoes, onions, cilantro, one tablespoon of olive oil and the juice from 1½ limes.

Add salt to taste and more limes or oil as needed.

You're done!

PEANUT

INGREDIENTS

½ cup peanut butter (creamy)

1 garlic clove (minced)

2 tbsp. soy sauce

2 tbsp. lime juice

2 tbsp. honey

¼ tsp. roasted chili flakes

¼ cup water

THE COOK

Mix all Ingredients in a blender.

You're done!

SPICY MANGO

INGREDIENTS

1 cup mango (diced)

1½ tbsp. Rice vinegar

1 tbsp. cilantro (coriander) (chopped)

1 bird's eye chili (seeded & chopped)

½ - 1 lime (juiced)

Pinch of salt

THE COOK

Mix all Ingredients in a blender.

You're done!

JOE'S HOT CHEESY DIP

INGREDIENTS

¼ cup chorizo sausage (fresh or dried)

1 small onion chopped

¼ pound mature cheddar

¼ pound cream cheese

4 tomatoes (roughly chopped)

Milk as needed

Pepper to taste

1 tbsp. cayenne pepper

1 cup cilantro/coriander (chopped)

½ scallion/spring onion (minced)

THE COOK

Cook the chorizo in a pan. Add the onions and cook until soft.

On low to medium heat, add the cream and cheddar cheeses to the pan.

Add milk to reach the desired thickness.

Add the tomatoes, cayenne, and scallions.

Top with cilantro.

You're done!

SALSA

INGREDIENTS

3 tomatoes (diced)

½ small onion (diced)

1 lime

1 bunch of cilantro

Olive oil

Salt & pepper

Extras

Sour cream

Cilantro

THE COOK

Mix the tomatoes, onions, cilantro, one tablespoon of olive oil and the juice from the lime in a bowl.

Add salt and pepper to taste and more limes or oil as needed.

You're done!

BARBEQUE

INGREDIENTS

2 cups tomato pasata

1 tbsp. paprika ½ sweet ½ smoked

1 tsp. cayenne pepper

¼ cup brown sugar

1 tbsp. chili powder

1 tbsp. salt

1 tbsp. pepper

1 tbsp. Worcester sauce

½ cup cider vinegar

6 garlic cloves chopped

3 tbsp olive oil

THE COOK

Combine all Ingredients in a saucepan.

Bring to the boil, and then simmer for 1 hour.

Served Chilled

YOGURT & DILL

INGREDIENTS

1 cup plain yoghurt

1 clove garlic

2 tsp. extra virgin olive oil

1-2 limes (juice)

2 tbsp. fresh dill (chopped)

THE COOK

Mix all Ingredients in a blender.
You're done!

NAHM JIM MAYO

INGREDIENTS

1½ tsp. fish sauce

1½ tsp. lime juice

1½ tsp. uncooked white rice

½ cup of chopped cilantro
(coriander)

½ cup of mayonnaise

1 tsp. chili flakes

THE COOK

Roast the rice in a dry frying pan or a dish in the oven
until it has browned.

Once it has cooled, use a pestle and mortar or spice
crusher to crush it to a semi-fine powder.

Mix the ground rice and the remaining nahm jim
mayo ingredients together

THANKS FOR BEING

AWESOME!

Printed in Great Britain
by Amazon